A
Pod
of

Killer Whales

THE MYSTERIOUS LIFE OF THE INTELLIGENT ORCA

BY VICKI LEÓN

LONDON TOWN PRESS

Jean-Michel Cousteau *presents*

Publishing Director
Jean-Michel Cousteau

Series Editor
Vicki León

A Pod of Killer Whales

Photographer
Jeff Foott

London Town Press
2026 Hilldale Drive
La Canada Flintridge, California 91011
www.LondonTownPress.com

Book design by Christy Hale
10 9 8 7 6 5 4 3 2

Printed in Malaysia

Distributed by Publishers Group West / Perseus

Library of Congress Cataloging-in-Publication Data
León, Vicki.
A pod of killer whales : the mysterious life of the intelligent
orca / by Vicki León.—2nd ed.
p. cm.—(Jean-Michel Cousteau presents)
Includes bibliographical references and index.
ISBN-13: 978-0-9766134-7-3 (softcover)
ISBN-10: 0-9766134-7-6 (softcover)
1. Killer whale—Juvenile literature. [1. Killer whale. 2. Whales.]
I. Title.
QL737.C432L46 2006
599.53'6—dc22
                                    2006027969

FRONT COVER: Extending its body up to the sky, a killer whale
spyhops to look at its surroundings. Especially if it's hunting,
the animal will often turn in a slow circle to see more.

TITLE PAGE: A male orca may weigh 400 pounds at birth
and reach 18,000 pounds as an adult. Females may weigh
8,000 pounds. In spite of their size, every move an orca makes
is graceful.

BACK COVER: Near British Columbia, the tall dorsal fin of an
adult orca is reflected in the calm waters. The dorsal fin on
males may grow to be six feet tall—and about half that size
for females.

Contents

▲ Eight killer whales swim in unison, their dorsal fins silhouetted against the golden waters of a Canadian sunset. The members of this pod are as close to a nap as orcas get. Always in motion, these animals never sleep deeply.

During my growing-up years on the Pacific coast, I never once saw a killer whale. I wasn't sure they really existed. In books and on television, killer whales looked like smooth black-and-white toys drawn by a kid my age.

My first glimpse of a live orca in the wild came much later, on a working trip to the Hawaiian Islands. There I saw a pod of killer whales, their dorsal fins silhouetted against the pink sunset.

Then I had the luck to visit the Vancouver Aquarium in British Columbia. Only then did I understand just how big and bold and in charge a killer whale is. As I leaned against the floor-to-ceiling display window, an animal bigger than my own bedroom glided up, then turned 180 degrees to skim under the colossal body of another killer whale. I watched for ages, admiring their huge sleekness, their powerful tails. When those orcas felt like it, the window on their side became wall-to-wall whale, watching me.

On that day began my fascination with killer whales, also called orcas from their scientific name, *Orcinus orca*. (In this book, you'll see both names.) Belonging to the order of cetaceans, the orca is a toothed whale closely related to the dolphin. A member of the Delphinidae family, it shares a similar body shape with dolphins. Most dolphins, however, look like shrimps compared to killer whales.

Sharks are probably the world's most famous predators—but even these great

KEY DIFFERENCES	
TOOTHED WHALES	**BALEEN WHALES**
One blowhole	Two blowholes
Sharp teeth to grab and tear prey	No teeth; brushy plates called baleen to strain plankton
Meat and fish-eaters that hunt live prey such as squid, fish, and seals in the sea or nearshore	Plankton eaters that strain microscopic plankton from the sea
Use "sonar" to echolocate	No echolocation
Asymmetrical skull	Symmetrical skull
70 species	11 species

▲ Whales are classified as either "toothed" or "baleen." Toothed whales include orcas, dolphins, and sperm whales. Baleen whales include gray whales, humpbacks, and blue whales.

fishes fear killer whales. For one thing, orcas are much bigger. Growing 20 to 30 feet long, they pack between four to nine tons (that's 18,000 pounds) of muscular power. Orcas swim tirelessly and can do bursts over 30 miles an hour, making them the fastest marine mammals. Fearless, intelligent, curious, and able to learn, killer whales are more than a match for any sea-going creature—and a few on land as well.

Orcas make their homes in all of the world's oceans. They tend to favor shallow waters close to shore, where most of their prey is found. The biggest concentration of killer whales (the best scientific guesses are somewhere between 70,000 to 180,000 animals) lives near Antarctica. Much smaller numbers are seen off Norway, Iceland, Russia, Japan, Papua New Guinea, and New Zealand. Orcas can be found in the Atlantic off North and South America and in the Pacific from Baja California to Alaska. They live in the waters around the Hawaiian islands, the Bahamas, and the British Isles, as well as in the Caribbean and Mediterranean.

The most stable and easily seen populations of killer whales are those found in Puget Sound from Washington state into British Columbia and Alaska. In four decades of field work, researchers have solved many mysteries about the orca by studying 500 animals in this region.

Because they are thinly scattered

around the globe, killer whale groups differ from one another. Orcas are what scientists call foraging specialists. Some populations go after schooling fish like herring or salmon, often working together to harvest them. Other populations pursue seals, turtles, seabirds, penguins, sharks, squid, rays, or porpoises. Some orcas tackle even larger targets, like elephant seals or gray whales. At times, killer whales travel to feed on a seasonal food supply, but they do not migrate from feeding to breeding grounds the way that gray whales do.

Killer whale groups also vary in their social organization. Some stay in one area, living in closely-knit groups called pods. Others are offshore loners, living mostly in the open ocean. Still other orcas called transients may form small pods that travel far and wide.

"When orcas surface to blow, they make a distinctive sound, a deep whuff!! that carries a long way. When they tail-lob or fall back into the water after a leap, the sound is sharper—more explosive."

—Jeff Foott

From flukes to dorsal fin

In the wild, orcas live as long as human beings. Male orcas can reach 50 years or more. Females outdo them, often surviving into their 70s or 80s. Clearly, a killer whale is built to last, its sturdy, streamlined body a wonder of nature.

That big head conceals a massive brain, four times the size of our own. Being overgrown dolphins themselves, it's no surprise they are smart. In the wild, older orcas teach the young, and continue to learn throughout their long lives.

An orca has a massive mouth, filled with 50 or more cone-shaped teeth that interlock, letting nothing escape. Killer whales use their teeth to grasp and tear, not to chew. Wide throats let them swallow most prey whole.

◀ Orcas are air-breathing mammals, not fish. When an orca expels warm air from its lungs, a cloud of steam spouts from the blowhole on its head. The blowhole acts like a big nostril. When the orca dives, it shuts tightly.

▼ Native peoples from Alaska to Peru have long admired the orca and honored its power and mystery in art, song, and story. The skull of an orca tells a story of its own. The whale's sharp teeth fit close together, to grab prey from seals to salmon.

The killer whale's eyes, found in front of the white eye-patches, see well above the water and below it. But this animal relies more on its super-keen hearing, often hunting in murky waters and at night. Besides having internal ears, the orca's oil-filled jawbone also picks up sound waves. Since sounds carry much further and faster underwater, the killer whale can hear its prey or its companions many miles away.

It's thought that orcas may have a geomagnetic sense that they use as a "map," the way that sharks and birds do.

On the top of the orca's head, this air-breathing mammal has one blowhole connecting to its lungs. After expelling stale air and sucking in fresh, the whale closes its blowhole before diving.

Unlike the bumpy hides of gray whales and humpbacks, the orca has an ultra-smooth skin, nicely padded with three to four inches of blubber. Orca skin cells in the top layer are large and flake off constantly as the animal swims. Just below that layer, the skin is hard and rubbery. This lets the animals move so smoothly through seawater that it flows in parallel layers around them. Scientists call this cool ability "laminar flow."

Orcas evolved into efficient, speedy swimmers with the help of body streamlining and smooth skin, unlike the scales and skins of cold-blooded sharks and other fishes. To keep their skin free of rough spots, some orcas rub themselves on gravel or pebbles found in the shallows of certain beaches. Other orca populations rub

◄ A small pod of killer whales glides along, diving and blowing. Each orca has a big dorsal fin. To human researchers, an orca's dorsal fin is like a fingerprint. No two are alike.

against masses of kelp. It's likely that killer whales use other methods as yet undiscovered by human observers.

The orca has paddle-shaped pectoral fins that help it steer. Its tail, divided into two flukes, provides power to move through the ocean.

Projecting from each orca's back is a stiff black dorsal fin, with an area of gray behind it called the saddle patch. Male dorsal fins can be six feet tall; the fin helps to steady the animal while swimming. Most dorsal fins stand upright but some orcas, both wild and captive, have dorsals that flop over. Scientists aren't sure why.

In the 1970s, Pacific Northwest orca researchers Michael Bigg and Graeme Ellis discovered that each dorsal fin and saddle patch had markings and notches unique to that animal. They began to photograph each whale and compile a database. These killer whale "fingerprints" now make it possible to identify thousands of individual animals. This in turn helps scientists understand orca family relationships, identify pod members, and track population sizes and movements. Researchers working elsewhere, like Dr. Ingrid Visser in the Antarctic, have followed their lead, establishing photo databases for other regions.

▲ The dorsal fin of one orca meets the tail of another. The shapely tail has two equal parts called flukes. Made of tough tissue, boneless, and flat, the tail can grow to be nine feet wide. Muscles in the orca's back help the tail power the animal through the sea, while the dorsal fin helps steer.

"On those rare days when the ocean is dead calm, orcas sometimes come up to blow without even breaking the surface tension of the water. Their sleek skin helps them do this. It's an amazing display of whale hydrodynamics in action."

—Jeff Foott

"Killer whale mothers are protective of their young, but not overly so. The calves are very curious and playful, especially when they get to be about two years old.

"How do I feel when I'm underwater with orcas? I respect their space and try to make myself as inconspicuous as possible. The whales have a very clear idea about me from their sonar. It's a powerful mechanism. When the whales are echolocating, the pulses hit my body with a force I can feel."

—Jeff Foott

Staying close to mom

Because orcas are huge, hungry predators, it's easy to suppose they are wandering hunters, patrolling the ocean alone. Some orcas do go solo. Thanks, however, to the long-term dedication of professional orca-watchers, it's well-established that many populations form lifelong family groups.

Not much is known about orca reproduction. Killer whales appear to be polygamous and do not form attachments to just one other whale. Scientists have yet to identify the father of any specific orca calf in the wild. Male whales, called bulls, may become sexually mature around 15 years, females or cows at 12–13 years.

Breeding can occur any time of year. In the Pacific Northwest, it is more frequent in late summer and fall. Around age 40, females stop bearing young but continue to guide and teach other pod members. Some cows apparently do not ever give birth. Only five percent of the whales in a pod are calves, a figure that shows how slowly orcas reproduce.

Once a cow becomes pregnant, the gestation period lasts somewhere between 15 and 17 months. It's almost always a

single birth. Other females, sometimes called "aunts" by researchers, gather around to help her. Weighing up to 400 pounds, the calf is born tail-first, open-eyed and vigorous. Instead of being black and white, the baby may have rosy-colored spots, due to the fact that its blubber layer is still thin. The eight foot long calf quickly swims below the belly of its mother to nurse. Because these whales have no lips and little ability to suck, the mother whale uses her mammary gland to squirt thick, fat-rich milk into her offspring's mouth.

The heart of killer whale society is the maternal group—a female orca and her offspring. Mother and calf bond tightly and stay within touching range. Calves may nurse for a year or two. Females bear young every three to ten years. After the mother has additional calves, her offspring, even the full-grown males, remain exceptionally close. They will spend their entire lives traveling and hunting with mom.

An orca calf is born toothless, like a human baby. It takes four months before it cuts top and bottom teeth. Only then does its mother begin to share bits of solid food.

As a maternal group grows, and the next generation of females has offspring, these closely related whales form a pod. A pod may represent as few as two maternal groups to as many as a dozen. Among fish-eating orcas, some pods grow very large—up to 50 whales. Pod members tend to do almost everything together: work and play, rest and rub on rocks, speed-swim and echolocate.

From time to time, orcas gather at favorite locales. These groupings, called superpods, present a remarkable sight. Observers have counted several hundred animals in some superpods. Scientists now believe that the animals gather to socialize and to mate with orcas outside their own pods.

Long-term studies in Puget Sound and

◀ Juvenile orcas can be very comical. They use kelp as toys and decorate their dorsal fins with it. They often play with their food. Sometimes an orca will hold a salmon in its mouth, popping it in and out many times before dining.

British Columbia show that most of the orcas belong to geographically defined communities. Although these animals spend a few months each year away from the area, they are often referred to as residents. These resident pods seem to have mutual respect for each other's watery territories.

Northernmost is the Alaskan community, where resident orcas have formed eleven pods that average about 20 animals in each. Extending from the southeast tip of Alaska down to the midway point of Vancouver Island, British Columbia, is the northern community. Sixteen pods and about 200 individual animals are known by name.

The southern community begins where the northern leaves off, running south into Puget Sound and along the coast of Washington. Its three pods struggle to maintain their numbers, now less than 90 whales.

Discovering that orca pods have home ranges was exciting enough. Then researchers discovered there are transient whales that don't fit the stay-at-home mold at all. Transients are shadowy wanderers, drifting in and out of resident communities and disappearing altogether for long periods.

Transient pods are small—two to seven animals. A few animals even go solo. These pods may travel great distances—up to 1,000 miles. They move quietly, vocalizing seldom. Transient orcas hunt marine mammals, while resident orcas live mostly on fish, so they can stay in the same area without competing. Transient orcas tend to visit the small bays and coves where seals, their favorite prey, frequently gather.

There are still big mysteries about orca societies. In 1988, a researcher discovered orcas that didn't quite fit the resident or transient pattern. Called offshore orcas, they travel in large pods, arriving in resident communities at unpredictable times. Even their eating habits are mysterious, although some clues point to shark as being their prey of choice.

▼ Although killer whales may look identical, they aren't. Researchers identify each individual by photographing their dorsal fins and saddle patches. Fins have different shapes, sizes, and scars. So do saddle patches, the greyish-white areas just behind the dorsal fin.

What could be more thrilling than boating among killer whales? For the boaters, it's the close encounter of a lifetime. But for the orcas, it can be stressful. Whale-watching boats, kayaks, and airplanes often jam the waters where orcas hunt, play, and rest. Boat motors make lots of racket underwater; the noise can greatly disturb orca hearing and sonar.

Orcas are curious and fearless. Human beings should let orcas approach if they choose to—not the other way around. Whale-watchers everywhere will benefit by respecting the animals and their wildness.

The curious, playful brain of the hunter

▼ A pert killer whale is caught at the tail end of a backdive breach, falling gracefully into the sea with the water streaming off its paddle-shaped pectoral fins, sometimes called flippers.

Like its cousin the dolphin, the killer whale has a delightful sense of play. The average orca can leap as high as a dolphin, but the majesty of its size makes the orca much more splashy, in every sense of the word.

The killer whale has a killer repertoire. Many whales breach, but few as acrobatically as the orca. Somehow it flings its five tons of black-and-white out of the water and 20 feet into the air. Afterwards, it falls into the sea with a crash, landing onto its belly, side, or back. Sometimes orcas spiral their

▶ Resident orcas often seek out special places to socialize and play. This quiet cove in British Columbia could be a play area for young orcas, full of kelp "toys." In the south Atlantic near the Crozet Archipelago, whales often rub against masses of living kelp, the same way that Canadian orcas rub against beach rocks.

▲ Young orcas love to play, and kelp is one of their "toys." This youngster uses the notch between its tail flukes to drag kelp through the water. By their teens, the bodies of killer whales are covered with scratches from years of boisterous chasing and roughhouse play.

bodies during a breach. At others, they flip in midair and re-enter the water, nose first. Orcas can even breach sideways!

Spyhopping is another crowd-pleasing move. To get a visual fix of its surroundings, an orca projects its huge body well out of the water. As it spyhops, the orca sometimes turns slowly in a 360-degree circle. Aquatic park trainers have used this natural tendency to persuade captive orcas to spin or "dance."

Orca playfulness has often been observed first-hand by veteran researchers like Juan Carlos López of Argentina. López had a habit of taking a daily walk with his family along a certain beach. One afternoon, an orca family showed up and started to swim parallel with the human family as they strolled. Not only did the orcas swim at the same speed, they stopped and started when the López family did.

It became a game. The López family experimented. They walked in a line, they walked side by side, they exchanged positions. Each time, the orcas imitated them. Finally, the leader of the pod slapped the sea several times with its tail flukes, as if to say, "OK—that's enough fun for now!" And the entire killer whale group swam off.

As it travels, a pod may spontaneously pick up speed until it zooms along at 30 miles per hour. This short burst of energy, called speed swimming or porpoising, may serve to break the monotony. How do the very young orcas keep up? They often ride just behind the mother's dorsal fin, "surfing" the wave off her back. At other times, the calf swims just below its mom's belly.

Orcas sometimes use speed swimming while hunting. An orca near the North or South Pole will speed-swim towards an iceberg where seals are resting. Just before

▶ An orca in a hurry zooms along the surface, spray coming off its dorsal fin. This behavior is called porpoising. Penguins, fish, dolphins, and porpoises also do it but killer whales are the biggest animals to porpoise. It is an energy-efficient way to travel at top speed, scientists have found.

▶ A bit like human beings, resident orcas of the northern community in British Columbia go to a favorite beach each summer. This area is called Robson Bight. At two protected beaches, killer whales take turns getting a rubdown from pebbles in the shallows.

diving under the iceberg, the orca flips its fins and flukes forward, sending a wave across the ice that sometimes washes their prey off the berg—and into the waiting mouth of another orca.

After feeding, some orca populations travel to favorite shoreline spots to socialize.

◄ These rocks have no algae or plant life growing on them, thanks to the "scrubbing" they get from killer whale activity.

The southern resident orcas of British Columbia favor Haro Strait as their core area. Northern resident orcas often visit Robson Bight, a place with special appeal. Almost every day in summer, killer whales come here to rub their bodies on the smooth stones of the shallows, scrubbing away dead skin and relieving itches at the same time.

Orcas, especially the more playful juveniles, often smack the water with their

▼ At Robson Bight, orcas wait their turn to rub their huge bodies against the rocky seafloor. Rubbing removes dead skin and helps the orcas keep sleek and speedy.

---

paddle-like flippers. They also tail-lob, beating their tail flukes against the surface. At times, killer whales produce these explosive sounds to stun or kill prey. At others, they seem to tail-lob and flipper-slap for noisy fun.

Killer whales living in pods synchronize much of their behavior with other pod members. They often rest together, letting one or two whales act as lookouts so that the dozing pod does not run into an obstacle. Their bodies almost touching, the orcas move at two to six miles at hour. They dive and blow in unison, murmuring to one another. Occasionally, their calm is broken by a frisky calf, demanding to be played with. It is usually answered by a scolding cry from its mother.

If orcas stopped moving and breathing, they would sink and drown. For this reason, they do not sleep deeply or long. They follow a 24-hour internal clock, resting and feeding during daylight and nighttime hours.

As foraging specialists, orcas have as many hunting methods as they do living

▲ The scars on the tail flukes of this gray whale were made by orca teeth, showing that it escaped at least one orca attack. Killer whales often hunt together when stalking larger animals. Even so, they fail to bring down prey quite a bit of the time.

arrangements. The method depends on the type of prey a given orca or group eats. Sometimes orcas eat items not on their regular menu. It's believed, however, that they eat new foods due to a lack of their regular prey. In other words, because they're hungry.

Fish-eating orcas often cooperate to hunt. To capture close-swimming schools like herring, orcas use a technique researchers call "carousel feeding." The orcas get under and around the fishes, circling the school like a merry-go-round. As they work, the circle gets tighter and closer to the surface. Then the orcas take turns breaching and slapping their tails, which stuns or kills some of the prey. They maintain the formation until each orca has fed.

To hunt salmon, Norwegian orcas form a line and "herd" the fishes into a narrow channel to trap them. The orcas take turns feeding while the rest keep the salmon from escaping.

New Zealand orcas specialize in hunting rays. As the rays rest on the bottom, concealed by mud, orcas nose them out and eat them. They go after rays hiding in shallow waters by burrowing their large heads into the mud.

Killer whales off Antarctica are flesh-eaters, mainly going after slower, easier to kill prey with lots of blubber. Sometimes they work in pairs or small groups but much more silently than fish-eating orcas. At times, they take turns to outwait a seal that has hidden in an underwater cave.

As any of these orcas would tell you if it could, it's hard work killing adult sea lions or elephant seals. These pinnipeds weigh thousands of pounds and have formidable

teeth and strength. Orcas team up to wear out this prey by ramming their victim from below. Sometimes they hit it with their tails until the animal is unconscious, then pull the pinniped underwater to drown it.

When attacking other whales, orcas collaborate. Even when they cooperate, they seldom take down a full-grown animal. Many whales survive orca attacks, as the scars on their bodies show. Sometimes orcas attack the calf of a gray whale, only to face its fierce mother. More than once, photographers have filmed orcas attacking a gray whale calf whose mother valiantly fights them—and loses.

The most dramatic hunting strategy used by orcas, first seen in the 1980s, takes place on a remote Argentinian peninsula. To hunt sea lion pups, some killer whales come ashore with the waves, beaching or stranding themselves on purpose to grab prey. This requires perfect timing, since the orca must be able to wiggle its massive body back out again. Pods continue to visit this peninsula, passing along their special skills to younger members.

In fact, we've learned that killer whales "practice" hunting in many ways so that their youngsters can learn the right moves. Argentine researcher López once saw an adult orca pluck a sea lion from the beach, then carry it offshore. The members of the orca pod played catch and release with the luckless animal for 45 minutes, then returned it. Although unhurt, that sea lion was a changed pinniped. From that moment on, at any hint of danger the sea lion hid himself in the bushes on shore instead of retreating into the water, as pinnipeds normally do.

"It was the fifth week I'd sat with my camera on a remote beach on the east coast of Argentina. The first orca attack on the seals was so sudden, I couldn't remember to press the shutter. It was all over in seconds.

"These steep Patagonian beachs have rocky bottoms, threaded with channels that lead towards the shore. By following the channels and stranding themselves, orcas can get near enough to grab prey. The momentum of the attack often brings them right up on the beach, where it takes several waves and a few hops to get back into the ocean."

—Jeff Foott

"Killer whales miss far more often than they succeed in these beach attacks. In fact, orcas prefer to go after fish in the surf, if it's available."
—Jeff Foott

"The orca's favorite targets? Elephant seal pups and sea lion pups. They are less able to defend themselves. The younger animals haven't learned where the killer whales can and cannot approach the shore."
—-Jeff Foott

▶ The first researcher to study wild orcas in Johnstone Strait, Dr. John Ford is an expert on killer whale vocalizations. Here he holds one of the hydrophones he's used to listen in on the orca pods of Washington and Canada.

Killer whale communication, in the wild and in captivity, has been studied for decades, pioneered by Dr. John Ford, Alexandra Morton, and others. Through these acoustic studies, the astonishing range and extent of killer whale "language" has come to light. The animals use two forms of communication: echolocation, a form of sonar, and vocalization.

When orcas navigate or search for food, they echolocate, sending out a stream of short, high-energy clicks or pulses. These pulses bounce off the objects and quickly return, giving the orca a "sound picture" of the size, speed, shape, and other details of the prey or object.

If they choose, orcas can send a burst of sound to stun fish prey—or even kill it. Human divers have reported being "buzzed" by the sonic pulses of dolphins and killer whales.

Although orcas have no vocal cords, they are very vocal. Besides echolocation, they have a big vocabulary of underwater sounds. They whistle, squeak, shriek, groan, gargle, and make high and low tones. Researchers divide these sounds into variable and discrete calls. Variable calls differ each time and seem to occur when socializing. Discrete calls sound the same each time.

Each pod of whales has five to 15 discrete calls that make up its own "dialect." Dialects are so distinctive that individual whales— even captive orcas—have been traced to their original pods. Dialects are passed down to succeeding generations also. Most

"One of the most exhilarating things I've ever seen is the way orcas move in unison. Sometimes a pod will get to a certain part of the shoreline, a headland, for instance, and begin speed swimming or breaching together in what looks like a mini-celebration."
—Jeff Foott

studies show that the calls remain the same for many generations.

No one knows just what killer whales are "saying" to each other. Their constant communication probably serves a number of purposes: to keep the pod together, to teach, to warn, to point out prey—and to communicate emotion, such as grief. Orcas have been heard to emit special cries when pod members or babies are lost.

The waters of the Puget Sound in the Pacific Northwest, where pod groups overlap and researchers have identified most individual residents, is an ideal base to study orca communication and dialects. Many orca vocalizations have been described and recorded—and a number can even be found at online websites.

Saving our orcas

Ancient human societies from New Zealand to South America revered killer whales. In Peru 1800 years ago, the Nazcan people made outline drawings in stone of giant orcas. In California and on the Channel Islands, the Chumash tribe honored the orca and carved its smiling image onto magical soapstone fetishes. The richest mythology came from the Tlingit and Haida tribes of the Pacific Northwest and Alaska. To them, the orca—called Skaana or Queet—was sometimes man's rescuer, sometimes a

monstrous half-bear, half-whale called the sea-grizzly. A favorite Tlingit character was Gondaquadate, the mythical chief of the orcas. A glimpse of him would bring good luck.

These stories, carved onto totem poles and woven into fabric, expressed underlying truths. For many cultures, the orca was a symbol of ferocity, strength, wisdom, and good fortune.

In later centuries, men started fearing killer whales, prompted by false tales of orca bloodthirstiness. Because of their remarkable hunting abilities, orcas also

▲ Orcas breach often but it's the younger whales that attempt the fanciest moves. Here, to the delight of nearby sailboaters, an animal does a breathtaking sideways breach.

◄ Many totem poles were carved by the Tlingit and Haida tribes living in British Columbia and Alaska. For centuries, they worshipped the killer whale for its courage and put its image on their totems, weavings, and pottery.

began to be hated by their human competitors. During the 19th and 20th centuries, whalers, seal hunters, and salmon fishermen called them "sea devils" and "savage sorts of Feegee fish." Along with other cetaceans, killer whales were slaughtered for their oil and meat. Whalers soon found, however, that it took 21 orcas to produce the oil found in one sperm whale. Orca meat was not tasty by human standards, either. Only Norwegian, Japanese, and Russian whalers seemed very interested in orcas; between 1938 and 1980, they killed over 3,000.

In the early 1960s, something happened that changed human fear into growing affection. Orcas were captured and exhibited to the public for the first time. The first two died shortly after capture; the third, dubbed "Moby Doll," lived about three months and became the first orca goodwill ambassador. Headlines and human curiosity made Moby Doll famous, and the legend of orca ferocity began to fade.

In 1965, an orca nicknamed Namu ended up in the Seattle Aquarium. It lived for a year and was seen by an even bigger audience. The animal's docility and

▼ "There is a very gentle, sensitive side to killer whales. You see it in the way they care for each other. And you feel it in their playful, tolerant, sometimes affectionate behavior toward us, their observers and captors."

—Jeff Foott

response to human coaching showed marine biologists and the general public that orcas were not the vicious killers they had been labeled.

Even though no one had proven that killer whales could survive very long in captivity, many aquatic parks now began live-capture programs. Within a decade, over 100 animals were captured and put on display at parks like Sea World and aquariums like the Vancouver Aquarium, where I saw my first orcas closeup.

There was very little known about wild orca behavior at the time. Aquatic professionals, however, soon saw that orcas needed daily social interaction as much as food. To act as substitutes for the orcas' family, trainers began to talk to their charges and touch the animals.

In 1972, the U.S. passed the Marine Mammals Protection Act, making it illegal to take orcas in U.S. waters. The whale capture industry moved to Canada and later, to Iceland, which outlawed the capture of whales in 1991. Studies in British Columbia soon began to reveal the intelligence of orcas and the complexity of their family life. As time went on, more orcas were

▼ In the wild, killer whales touch and communicate as they rest, play, and travel in family groups called pods. In captivity, a trainer is the only "family" an orca has. Trainers reward orcas with massages, praise, and tongue-rubs like this one.

killed during capture; more of them died in captivity; and more people became concerned about removing these animals from the wild.

In 1993, a film called "Free Willy" became a huge hit worldwide, especially with schoolchildren. What happened after the movie was more touching than the film itself. The film's "star," an orca named Keiko, lived in a small squalid tank within a Mexican amusement park. With the

generous support of donors, the Free Willy Keiko Foundation came into being and raised funds for a rehabilitation facility. Years were spent healing and preparing the animal for its return to the wild. When Keiko finally learned to hunt on its own, it was freed. It promptly took a month-long swim from Iceland to Norway.

The affection that Keiko, an "ambassador of the wild," awakened in children and their parents made the save-the-whale movement a global issue. Because of the outcry over orcas and other cetaceans, endangered whale species began to win legal protection from the world's nations.

Today, fewer than 50 orcas remain in captivity and on display. Despite expert medical attention and caring human trainers, only a handful of orcas have survived more than 20 years in captivity. Compared to the long life that killer whales enjoy in the wild, that isn't much.

Many people feel that human beings have no right to remove orcas from their families and almost certainly shorten their life expectancy, just to provide entertainment. Others argue that the educational value of seeing orcas justifies the captivity of a few.

I'm pulled both ways. I love seeing killer whales in the wild. But I also realize that my deep admiration for these creatures began when I saw them in captive settings—the same way that countless other people have fallen for orcas.

Marine parks and aquariums with orcas do many positive things. Their orcas give wonder to children, insights to the rest of us, and new knowledge to science. If these smart, long-lived creatures and their off-

▲ Killer whales are masters at breaching and do it often. They leap out of the water, soaring as high as a two-story building. They do back dives, bellyflops, and even cartwheels. Their submarine-shaped bodies are made for acrobatics.

spring are to be kept, however, their lives must not be wasted. Just as has been done with zoos, the public needs to insist on sensitive treatment, generous enclosures, humane conditions, and down time, away from visitors, for captive orcas.

In the 21st century, some whale species, like the grays and the humpbacks, have rebounded from threatened extinction. Not so the killer whale. More threats to its wild populations have surfaced, some of them due to the orca preference for nearshore hunting.

Noise pollution from human activity is a major peril. Since orcas depend on sonar and underwater vocalizations, boat engine noise can disturb them—especially in places where whale-watching brings millions of people onto the water each year. The U.S. Navy's use of low-frequency, high-decibel sonar has also been highly criticized for the damage it may be doing to the sonar systems of orcas and dolphins.

In 1993, another problem arose: the use of underwater harassment devices to scare off seals. The noise drove killer whales from an important feeding area in Canada. Six years later, when the acoustic devices were removed, the orcas returned.

Chemical pollution is another threat. As predators at the top of their food chain, orcas absorb massive amounts of dioxin and other toxins in their prey food. Killer whales are the most PCB-contaminated creatures on the planet. Worse yet, their calves absorb these toxins before birth and through their mother's milk.

For fish-eating orcas, starvation is another stark reality. Wild salmon are in steep decline in the U.S., Canada, Norway,

and elsewhere. Salmon farms have sprung up to replace wild fish, but have created major problems of their own. These commercial farms produce more than farmed salmon. They are overrun with millions of sea lice, parasites that escape and gobble tiny wild salmon before they can reproduce.

In our crowded, polluted world, these factors have put immense pressure on killer whale populations. In some places, their status is threatened. The much-admired pods of the southern resident population off Washington and British Columbia were listed as endangered in 2005.

Can we undo the damage? Yes, if you and I and millions of other people start making common-sense changes today and hold to them.

It's critical that we become better caretakers of our land and water resources, from our baby salmon to our giant orcas. That means telling political representatives at every level to stop the dumping of toxins into the ocean. To stop building dams on rivers so that wild salmon numbers regain their strength. To insist on safeguards for commercial salmon farms so that wild and farmed salmon don't interbreed or spread diseases and parasites.

There are other useful steps anyone can take. Join global groups like the Whale and Dolphin Conservation Society. Take part in hands-on research expeditions from Earthwatch, as I have. "Adopt" orcas through the Whale Museum and many other organizations. Educate yourself and others about respectful orca-watching, whether it's from a ship, kayak, or the shore. Get more educated through the stirring films

and photos made by wildlife professionals like Jeff Foott.

It's not too late to make things better. If we do nothing else, you and I, let us give the living orca, not just its memory, to future generations.

▲ Pod members often swim in unison like these two whales. Their eyes are clearly visible, just in front of the white eye patch on their bodies.

Secrets of killer whales

- Killer whales are picky eaters. When they take down a gray whale calf, they gobble the tongue and blubber first. When they catch penguins, they eat everything except the skin and feathers.

- Most sea creatures fear orcas. Even salmon have been seen hiding against a boat when killer whales come near.

- An orca on a seal hunt sometimes swims upside-down, looking up at the surface to spot the familiar shape of its prey.

- Killer whales receive sound through their lower jawbone as well as their ears. They can hear underwater calls up to 15 miles away.

- Orca moms keep their calves close. A calf swims right under her belly, where it can nurse when it likes.

- A baby orca drinks milk as thick as cream. In its first few weeks, it may nurse 20 times an hour!

- Some killer whales vocalize non-stop. Other orcas are often silent. That helps them sneak up on larger, more wary prey.

- Male orcas may live to be 50 in the wild; most never leave their mothers but travel and hunt in her pod or group.

- Female killer whales give birth to calves until they are 40. After that, they seem to act as "wise grandmothers" to the pod.

- Dolphins and killer whales are cousins but orcas are ten times heavier. Killer whales can jump higher and swim faster. One orca, timed at 34.5 miles per hour, made the Guinness Book as the world's fastest marine mammal.

◄ For centuries, fishermen and hunters have competed with orcas, and sometimes killed them, over salmon and seals. Nevertheless, orcas do not fear human beings. These days, some fishing boats run orca-watching tours instead of fishing. Many busy charters like this one operate out of Puget Sound, British Columbia, and Alaska.

Glossary

Baleen. A brushy plate that hangs from the upper jaw of whales like the humpback and strains tiny particles of food from seawater. Baleen whales are toothless; orcas and others are toothed whales.

Blowhole. The breathing hole on top of an orca's head that connects to its lungs. Killer whales have one blowhole, baleen whales have two.

Breaching. An above-water behavior often done by orcas. The animal leaps high into the air or sometimes sideways, landing with a big splash.

Carousel feeding. A cooperative behavior among some orcas that hunt fish species swimming in tight schools, like herring. Orcas force the fish upward into a merry-go-round motion. Then the whales take turns feeding.

Cetacean. One of the species in the Cetacean order of mammals. Killer whales are cetaceans. So are dolphins and blue whales.

Community. The name given to all the killer whale pods based in the same geographic area.

Dialect. The special calls and vocalizations used between members of an orca pod. Each pod has a different "dialect" that is passed on to new generations.

Discrete call. Vocalizations made by orcas that sound exactly the same each time they are made.

Dorsal fin. Large triangle-shaped fin on the back of an orca that keeps it steady while swimming.

Echolocation. Like sonar on a submarine, orcas "see" in dark murky water by sending out pulses or echoes and listening as they come back. In this way, orcas learn the size and shape of prey and objects.

Fluke. The powerful tail of an orca is divided into two flat sections, called flukes. Other whale species also have tail flukes.

Geomagnetism. A "guidance system" used by birds, sharks, and possibly by orcas in their underwater travels. This sense uses the earth's magnetic lines of force as a map.

Laminar flow. An adaptation that lets the sleek, two-layered skin of killer whales move smoothly through the sea.

Pod, superpod. A group of orcas that remain together all their lives. A pod is made up of two to 12 maternal groups of females and their offspring. Superpods occur when pods join briefly to socialize or to mate.

Polygamous. Killer whales are polygamous, meaning males and females do not have lifelong partners but breed with more than one whale during their lives.

Saddle patch. The grey or white patch of skin directly behind an orca's dorsal fin. Each patch is slightly different, making it a useful way for human beings to tell orcas apart.

Spyhopping. A cetacean behavior, common among orcas. The animal raises its body vertically into the air to look around at its surroundings.

Stranding. Orcas and other whales sometimes get disoriented and come ashore. Unable to return to deep water, they may die. In certain areas, however, orcas strand themselves on purpose to hunt sea lions. Taught how by other orcas, they get away safely.

Tail-lobbing. Also called lobtailing, this behavior is common among orcas. In play, or sometimes to stun prey, the animals explosively slap their tails against the surface of the water.

Variable call. Vocalizations made by orcas that are different each time. Researchers think variable calls are used when whales socialize.

About the author

Vicki León has written other books in this series, including *A Raft of Sea Otters*, *A Colony of Seals*, and *A Rainbow of Parrots*.

About the photographer

Jeff Foott, an accomplished photographer, cinematographer, and naturalist, lives in the West, close to the wildlife he admires and photographs so eloquently. Nominated for an Emmy for his television film on orcas, he has also captured other awards for his films on sea otters, bighorn sheep, and manatees. His photographs appear in countless books, magazines, and calendars.

Special thanks

To the researchers and advocates who've devoted their lives to orcas, including Ken Balcomb; Alan Baldridge and the Hopkins Marine Station of Stanford University; Dr. Michael Bigg; the Center for Whale Research at Friday Harbor, Washington; Dr. Richard Murphy of the Ocean Futures Society; Graeme Ellis; Dr. John Ford; Juan Carlos López; Alexandra Morton; and Dr. Ingrid Visser.

Where to see orcas

In the wild: Orcas are legally protected in many parts of the world. It's natural to want to see or photograph them up close, but human interference can seriously disturb their daily life. Sometimes they can be seen off the Pacific coast and from the ferries that ply the waters of Puget Sound. Whale-watching from charter boats, now available in 87 countries, including the U.S. and Canada, attracts over 9 million people a year. At times the popularity of whale-watching turns places like Johnstone Strait in British Columbia into crowded, noisy traffic jams.

Two gentler ways to experience orcas: Volunteer for one of the research expeditions, through Earthwatch Institute, the Center for Whale Research, and others. Or choose trips that minimize impact on the animals, such as those run by the Whale and Dolphin Conservation Society.

In captivity: Many marine parks and aquaria no longer display orcas. Killer whales can still be seen, however, at the three Sea Worlds in California, Texas, and Florida; at four Japanese aquatic parks; and at facilities in France, Spain, and Argentina.

▶ At an aquatic park, a trainer shows a small boy how captive orcas are fed. In the wild, most orcas would not eat a tiny piece of dead fish. Their three-inch-long teeth are designed to grab bigger, live prey.

Helping organizations & good websites

- Free Willy Keiko Foundation, 300 Broadway, Suite 28, San Francisco, CA 94133. Begun as the organization that rescued Keiko, the "Free Willy" orca, the foundation now devotes its resources to help other whales, both wild and captive. Authoritative source on everything about Keiko. (www.keiko.com)
- Earthwatch Institute, 3 Clock Tower Place, #100, Maynard MA 01754. Superb organization that fields volunteers (kids, teens, and teachers, too) and funds projects like Ken Balcomb's orca identification study; inspiring website. (www.earthwatch.org)
- The Center for Whale Research, PO Box 1577, Friday Harbor WA 98250. Great photos, video, and info from the center where decades-long studies of area orcas and pods are carried out by Ken Balcomb. (www.whaleresearch.org)
- Whale Museum, 62 First St. N, PO Box 945, Friday Harbor WA 98250. On Orcas Island, excellent museum with an array of programs from Adopt an Orca to the Whale Hotline. Fascinating website lets you see where pods and individual orcas pop up. (www.whalemuseum.org)
- Raincoast Research Society, Simoon Sound, British Columbia, Canada V0P 1SO. Lots to read: Alexandra Morton's brilliant fieldwork with orcas, info on the troubled salmon farming industry. Amazing photos and details about her books. (www.raincoastresearch.org)
- Whale and Dolphin Conservation Society, Wildlife Centre, Moray Firth, Scotland. A global voice for the protection of whales and dolphins, the WDCS fields a variety of orca research programs. (www.wdcs.org) Good Australasia site also at (www.wdcs.org.au)
- Orca Research Trust, PO Box 1233, Whangarei, New Zealand. The website of Dr. Ingrid Visser, key researcher on South Pacific orcas in Antarctica. If you want to hear wild orca sound effects, this is the place. (www.orcaresearch.org)
- National Geographic. Up-to-date news bulletins on orcas at this entertaining, valuable website. (www.nationalgeographic.com)

To learn more

Books

These recommended books have important information about orca lives and about threats to their survival.

- *Listening to Whales: What the Orcas Have Taught Us*, by Alexandra Morton. (Ballantine Books 2002). Fascinating, detailed look at wild (and captive) orcas by an eloquent, eminent researcher and activist. Her children's book *Siwiti* is also a winner.
- *Killer Whales of the World*, by Robin Baird. (Voyageur Press 2002). Oversized pictorial with stirring photos, excellent range maps and text.
- *Killer Whales*, by Mark Carwardine. (DK/BBC Worldwide 2001). Well-written, generously illustrated book.
- *Killer Whales*, by John Ford, Graeme Ellis, and Kenneth Balcomb. University of British Columbia Press, 2000. Impressive, troubling statistics and facts from key orca researchers.

Magazines

- "Investigating a Killer," by Douglas Chadwick, photos by Flip Nicklin. National Geographic magazine, April 2005 issue.

DVDs, videos & films

- "Killer Whales, Wolves of the Sea." National Geographic 1993. VHS format, 1 hour. Remarkable sequences of orca hunts and behaviors in four oceans of the world.
- "Killer Whales of the Pacific Northwest." Vancouver Aquarium Marine Science Centre, 1989. VHS format, 35 minutes. Older documentary, still a good video for younger kids.
- "Free Willy." Warner Brothers film, 1993. VHS and DVD format, 112 minutes. This powerful film, "starring" a captive orca at a Mexico City facility, aroused intense interest in whales and public outrage at the abusive conditions of this captive. The Free Willy Keiko Foundation, headed by Jean-Michel Cousteau, helped rescue and rehabilitate the orca for its eventual release into the open ocean.
- "Orca: Killer Whale or Gentle Giant?" Whale Museum Store (available at their website). DVD format, 26 minutes. Unusual footage of a birth at sea, a salmon hunt, and more.
- "Orca Survey." Great footage and vocals of the Pacific Northwest orcas. VHS, 60 minutes. Available from the Center for Whale Research, address given under Helping Organizations.

Index

Photographs are numbered in **boldface** and follow the print references after **PP** (photo page).